Longman Test Practice Kits

English

Key Stage 2

Alan Gardiner

Longman

Series editors
Geoff Black and Stuart Wall

Titles available

Key Stage 1
English
Mathematics

Key Stage 2
English
Mathematics
Science

Key Stage 3
English
Mathematics
Science

Pearson Education Limited
Edinburgh Gate
Harlow
CM20 2JE
England
and associated companies throughout the world

First published 1998
Second impression 1999

ISBN 0582 31575-1

British Library Cataloguing-in-Publication Data
A catalogue record for this book is available from the British Library.

Set by 34 in 13/19pt Frutiger light

Printed in Great Britain by Henry Ling Limited, at the Dorset Press,
Dorchester, Dorset

Table of contents

Acknowledgements

We are grateful to Macmillan Press Ltd for permission to reproduce the poem 'Two's Company' from *Rhyme and Rhythm – Yellow Book* by Gibson and Wilson (1965).

The Key Stage 2 National Tests

How they work

- During Years 3–6 your child will be studying English, Mathematics and Science as part of Key Stage 2 of the National Curriculum. At the end of Year 6 (at age 11) your child will take National Tests in each of these subjects.
- The National Curriculum for English is divided into three parts, known as Attainment Targets:

  1 Speaking and Listening
  2 Reading
  3 Writing, including handwriting and spelling.

  The National Tests assess Attainment Targets 2 and 3.
- These written National Tests (sometimes called SATs) will take place in May of Year 6. Your child will take them in his or her own school, but they will be marked by examiners from outside the school.
- Most children will take three papers in English:

  1 Reading Test – 45 minutes plus 15 minutes reading time
  2 Writing Test – 45 minutes plus 15 minutes planning time
  3 Spelling and Handwriting Test – 15 minutes.

- You will receive the results of your child's National Test by the end of July. Along with these Test results, you will receive the results of assessments made by your child's teacher in the classroom.
- You will find your child's results are expressed as a **Level** for both the National Tests and the Teacher Assessment.
- You will receive a summary of the Key Stage 2 results achieved by all the other pupils in your child's school, and for all pupils nationally. You will then be able to check your child's progress against other pupils of the same age.

Levels of achievement

Each subject is divided into Levels 1–6 at Key Stage 2. You can see from the table below that your child is expected to reach Level 4 by the end of Key Stage 2.

☐ Exceptional performance	Level 6	☐
▨ Exceeded targets for age group	Level 5	▨
⊟ Achieved targets for age group	Level 4	⊟
■ Working towards targets for age group	Level 3	■
	Level 2	■
	Level 1	■

Table 1. Levels of achievement (Key Stage 2)

Levels of entry

Most children will take the three papers for Levels 3–5 in English. Exceptionally able pupils may also take an Extension Paper with Level 6 questions.

This book concentrates on Levels 3–5, and presents questions of the type your child can expect to face in the actual examination.

Using this book

Part 1 Self-check revision

Part 1 (pages 4–29) of this book provides a brief outline of some important topics relevant to Key Stage 2 English. Studying these topics will help your child to prepare for the National Tests. To make this revision more interesting, there are short-answer questions from time to time to help your child check his or her knowledge and understanding. Answers to all these questions can be found at the end of Part 1 (see pages 28–29).

Part 2 Test practice papers

Part 2 (pages 30–65) includes the following:

- **Test Practice Papers**   Three full Test Practice Papers
- **Answers and Mark Scheme**   Answers to the Test questions, and guidance on awarding marks
- **Examiner's Tips**   Helpful advice from the examiner to help improve your child's marks
- **Marking Grid**   How to calculate and interpret your child's overall score

PART 1

Self-check revision

In this section you will find a brief, easy to use review of the key facts that your child is expected to know for their National Test.

To help make your child's revision more active and interesting, short-answer questions have been set on most of the ten topic areas. Answers to these questions can be found at the end of Part 1 (pages 28–29).

After you have revised a topic with your child, and completed the questions set on that topic, place a tick in the appropriate box in the progress chart below. This will help you to keep a record of your child's progress. It will be best if your child revises all the topics before they begin the Test Practice Papers in Part 2 of this book.

Revision progress chart

	Topic	Tick when revised
1	**Grammar: parts of speech**	
1.1	Nouns	
1.2	Pronouns	
1.3	Adjectives	
1.4	Verbs	
1.5	Adverbs	
1.6	Conjunctions	
1.7	Prepositions	
1.8	Self-check exercise	
2	**Grammar: sentences**	
2.1	What is a sentence?	
2.2	Subject	
2.3	Verb	
2.4	Other sentences	
2.5	Self-check exercise	
3	**Punctuation: capital letters, full stops, question marks and exclamation marks**	
3.1	Capital letters	
3.2	Full stops	
3.3	Question marks	
3.4	Exclamation marks	
3.5	Self-check exercise	

Grammar: parts of speech

1.1 Nouns

Nouns tell us the **names** of objects, people, places, feelings and ideas.
These words are all nouns:

chair   mountain   Sally
girl   excitement France

1.2 Pronouns

Pronouns **take the place of nouns**. They are used instead of nouns.
In the piece of writing below, some pronouns are printed in bold but
others have been left out. Can you fill in the blanks?

This watch is very special to **me**. **1**____ was given to **me** by
my grandfather. **2**____ wore **it** when **he** sailed around
the world on a yacht. **3**____ like showing **it** to my friends.

1.3 Adjectives

Adjectives **describe nouns**:

a **new** toy
a **beautiful** garden
a **nice** feeling

Can you think of *two* adjectives to describe the boy in the picture
below, and *two* different adjectives to describe his mother?

The boy is **4**_____
and **5**_____

His mother is **6**_____
and **7**_____

Answers can be found on page 28

1.4 Verbs

Verbs are words which refer to **actions**. They are sometimes known as 'doing' words. The sentence below is about the boy in the picture on the opposite page. The first verb is in bold but the others have been left out. Can you fill them in?

> Johnny **tried to** 8_____ across the stream, but he
> 9_____ on the muddy bank and 10_____ in
> the water.

1.5 Adverbs

Adverbs **tell us more about actions:**

> I **nearly** missed the train. I only caught it because I ran
> **quickly** all the way to the station.

Most adverbs are made by adding **-ly** to the ends of adjectives:

> near + ly = nearly
> quick + ly = quickly

1.6 Conjunctions

Conjunctions are **joining** words. They join together the different parts of a sentence. Write in the spaces the conjunctions that could be used to join this sentence together:

> Mr Jones tried very hard to pass his driving test
> 11_____ he failed 12_____ he forgot to put his
> seat-belt on.

1.7 Prepositions

Prepositions tell us **what one person or thing has to do with another person or thing**. Usually they show **where** something is:

> The cat came **into** the room. It jumped **onto** the
> window-sill then hid **behind** the sofa.

Answers can be found on page 28

1.8 Self-check exercise

Fill in the blanks in this table.

Noun	Adjective	Adverb
joy	joyful	joyfully
13_____	**14**_____	happily
anger	**15**_____	**16**_____
17_____	frightening	**18**_____
19_____	**20**_____	courageously

Answers can be found on page 28

topic **2**

Grammar: sentences

2.1 What is a sentence?

A sentence is a group of words which can stand by itself and make sense. Sentences begin with a capital letter and most end with a full stop, though some sentences end with a question mark or an exclamation mark. Usually, sentences are only proper sentences if they have a **subject** and a **verb**.

2.2 Subject

To find the subject of a sentence, ask yourself:

Who or what is the sentence about?

In the first two sentences below, the subject is shown. Write the subjects of the other sentences in the spaces.

Sentence	Subject
Susan climbed the tree.	Susan
Greece can be very hot in the summer.	Greece
Mary is Colin's sister.	**1**_____
The tree was blown down by the wind.	**2**_____
The shop sold computer games.	**3**_____

The subject can usually be found at the *beginning* of the sentence, but this is not always the case. Write the subjects of the sentences below in the spaces.

Sentence	Subject
After tossing and turning for two hours, Paul finally went to sleep.	**4**_____
At eight o'clock the next morning he woke up.	**5**_____
Realizing he was awake, his little sister came into the room.	**6**_____

Answers can be found on page 28

9

2.3 Verb

The verb in a sentence tells us what something is doing or being.
Write out the verbs in the spaces below.

Sentence	Verb
Peter went to the circus.	went
The dog barked very loudly.	barked
My uncle swam the English Channel.	**7** _____
The rain fell heavily.	**8** _____
She is nine years old.	**9** _____

2.4 Other sentences

Certain types of sentences do not need a subject or a verb.
These include:

- **Exclamations**   *Oh dear! My goodness!*
- **Commands**   These have a verb but do not have a subject:
                          Sit down! Be quiet!
- **Greetings, farewells, etc.**   *Hello. Good morning. Goodbye.*
- **Answers to questions**   How old are you?
                          Ten.

2.5 Self-check exercise

Some of the sentences below are correct. Others are incorrect, either
because they have *no subject* or because they have *no verb*. Write the
correct description of each sentence in the column headed Comment.
Remember to ask yourself the following questions:

   Does the sentence make sense?
   Does it have a subject?
   Does it have a verb?

Answers can be found on page 28

Sentence	Comment
Jumped six feet into the air	No subject
I saw Teresa yesterday.	Correct
Houses with large gardens.	No verb
Jim spoke to the policeman.	**10** _____
The three monkeys.	**11** _____
Goodnight.	**12** _____
Imran, Jennifer and Michael.	**13** _____
Walking towards the river.	**14** _____
Running up the hill.	**15** _____
I flew in an aeroplane last week.	**16** _____
John, fifteen years old but already nearly six feet tall.	**17** _____
Go to bed!	**18** _____
Will rise at seven o'clock this morning and set at eight o'clock this evening.	**19** _____
Flowers grow.	**20** _____

Answers can be found on page 28

11

Punctuation: capital letters, full stops, question marks and exclamation marks

3.1 Capital letters

Capital letters are used:
- at the beginning of every sentence
- for the names of people, places, streets, roads and buildings
- for the days of the week, months of the year and special days such as Christmas Day
- for the titles of books, plays, films, etc.
- for the word **I**, which should never be written as a small letter.

In the piece of writing below, eight words have been written incorrectly. They should all begin with capital letters. Write the eight words in the spaces.

> i am looking forward to my birthday on august 6th.
> this year my birthday falls on a sunday. i will be having a
> party on that day and have invited christopher, laura
> and robert.

The eight words that should have capital letters are:

1 _____   **5** _____

2 _____   **6** _____

3 _____   **7** _____

4 _____   **8** _____

3.2 Full stops

Full stops are used to mark **the end of a sentence**.

They can also be used in **abbreviations**. Do you know the meaning of the following abbreviations? Write them in the spaces.

m.p.h. **9** _____

Mr. **10** _____

Dr. **11** _____

Answers can be found on page 28

Some abbreviations are used so much that the full stops are usually left out. Write down the meanings of these abbreviations:

UFO   **12** _____

MP   **13** _____

3.3 Question marks

Some sentences end not with full stops but with question marks. (You should never end a sentence with both.) When a sentence asks a question, end it with a question mark:

How old are you?

If a sentence does not actually ask a question, but instead describes a question that somebody has asked, the sentence ends with a full stop:

He asked me how old I was.

Each of the sentences below should end with a full stop or a question mark. Write the correct punctuation mark in the space provided.

What is the time	**14** _____
I asked her where she was going	**15** _____
I wondered where you were	**16** _____
Where are you	**17** _____

3.4 Exclamation marks

Another way of ending a sentence is with an exclamation mark. These are used when someone shouts, or when a strong emotion such as shock or anger is being expressed:

'Go away!' he cried.

'How dare you!'

3.5 Self-check exercise

Which punctuation mark (full stop, question mark or exclamation mark) should each of these sentences end with?

I asked for some money	**18** _____
Help	**19** _____
Where have you been all day	**20** _____

Answers can be found on page 28

Punctuation: commas, inverted commas and apostrophes

4.1 Commas

Commas are usually used to make sentences easier to read or to understand. They are like pauses for breath in the middle of a sentence. Try reading the following sentence out loud without stopping.

> Kerry who was nearly nine had two favourite dresses a red one and a blue one.

This sentence needs commas to slow it down and make it easier to read. Commas could be placed after *three* of the words in the sentence. What are they?

1_____   **2**_____   **3**_____

Commas are also used between words in a **list**. Remember, though, that the last two items in a list are usually joined by **and**, which means a comma is not needed between them.

Which words in the following sentence need a comma after them?

> At the shop she bought apples oranges bananas grapes and two juicy pears.

The words are: **4**_____   **5**_____

6_____

4.2 Inverted commas

These are also known as **speech marks** or **quotation marks**. They are used **around words that are actually spoken**:

> 'I will see you tomorrow,' he said.

They can also be used around the **titles** of books, films, etc.:

> I went to see 'Star Wars' on Saturday.

Answers can be found on page 28

14

4.3 Apostrophes

Try to remember that not all words that end in *s* need an apostrophe. In fact they are only needed on *two* occasions:

1 to show ownership (when something belongs to somebody)
2 to show that letters are missing.

Showing ownership

Here is a simple way to make sure that you always put an apostrophe in the right place:

    1 Ask yourself, 'Who is the owner?'
    2 Put the apostrophe after the *last letter* of the owner's name.

Look at this example:

    Sarah's computer

    Who is the owner? Sarah.
    What is the last letter of the owner's name?
      The last letter of Sarah is *h*.
    Where does the apostrophe go? After the *h*

Here are a few more examples:

	Who is the owner?	*Where does the apostrophe go?*
the policeman's helmet	the policeman	after the *n*
the children's toys	the children	after the *n*
the boy's books (= the books belonging to *one* boy)	the boy	after the *y*
the boys' books (= the books belonging to *two* boys)	the boys	after the *s*

Now copy out in the spaces provided the words that have been shown in bold below, putting apostrophes in the right places.

7 **Wendys** bicycle _____

8 my **friends** book _____

9 **womens** clothes _____

10 the **thieves** getaway car _____

11 **Mr. Osbornes** shop _____

12 the **pupils** mothers and fathers _____

13 my **fathers** friends _____

14 **Jamess** pencil case _____

Showing that letters are missing

Put the apostrophe where the missing letters would normally be:

do not	becomes	**don't**
we will	becomes	**we'll**

Copy out the following words, putting apostrophes in the correct places:

youre	**15** _____		Im	**18** _____
cant	**16** _____		arent	**19** _____
didnt	**17** _____		isnt	**20** _____

its and it's – a special case

When **it's** means **it is** or **it has**, then use an apostrophe:

It's raining.

When **its** means **belonging to it**, you do not need an apostrophe:

The dog wagged its tail.

Answers can be found on page 28

Spelling

5.1 How words sound

Think about the different sounds that go to make up a word.
The word **unlikely**, for example, is made up of three sounds:

> un + like + ly = unlikely

It sometimes helps to break down a word in this way and spell it one
part at a time. Break down these words in the same way:

footballer   **1**_____

inevitable   **2**_____

5.2 Groups of letters

The more you read and write, the more you will get used to seeing and
using certain groups of letters which often go together and which are
always spelt the same. Here are some examples:

dis   These letters are often attached to the beginnings
of words:

> dis + agree = disagree   (*not* 'dissagree')
> dis + appear = disappear (*not* 'dissappear')

Which of the two spellings below is correct? Write the correct spelling in
the space.

disslike

dislike

3_____

al   These letters are also attached to the beginnings of
words:

> al + ways   = always   (*not* 'allways')
> al + together = altogether   (*not* 'alltogether')

Answers can be found on page 28

ful These letters are also added to the ends of words:

> wonder + ful = wonderful   (*not* 'wonderfull')
> hand + ful = handful   (*not* 'handfull')

ph These letters are often used together to make an *f* sound:

> photograph
> elephant

ch These letters are often used together to make a *k* sound:

> school
> Christmas

5.3 Keep a list

Keep a list of words that you spell incorrectly. Try to use the words when you write so that you get into the habit of spelling them correctly.

Test yourself in the following way:
- *Look* at the word.
- *Say* the spelling out loud.
- *Cover* the word so you cannot see it.
- *Write* it down.

5.4 Self-check exercise

There are 17 spelling mistakes in the piece of writing below. Find the mistakes and write the correct spellings in the spaces on page 19.

> It wass a beautifull day. The sun was shineing brightley and their was not a cloud to be seen. Suddenly the telefone rang. My mum ansered it. It was my farther. He works in a kemist's shop but he was ringing to say that his boss had sed he could finish werk erly. My dad said we should all meat at the trian station and then go

Answers can be found on page 28

toogether to the zoo. I have been to the zoo lots of times and I allways love goeing there.

4 _____	10 _____	16 _____
5 _____	11 _____	17 _____
6 _____	12 _____	18 _____
7 _____	13 _____	19 _____
8 _____	14 _____	20 _____
9 _____	15 _____	

Answers can be found on page 28

Handwriting

Here are some reminders about some of the features of good handwriting.

6.1 Letters should be the correct size

Capital letters should be bigger than ordinary (small) letters. No letters should be unusually large or unusually small when compared with other letters. Try to keep the size of your letters even and regular.

6.2 Avoid slanted handwriting

Try to keep your letters upright rather than sloping to the right or to the left.

6.3 Avoid 'squeezing' words

Do not leave yourself so little room at the end of a line that you have to squeeze the letters of the last word into a tiny space. Instead, begin the word on a new line.

6.4 Keep regular spaces between words

Keep the spaces between words the same. Do not have some words that are very close together and others that are very far apart.

6.5 Ways of improving your handwriting

Good handwriting comes with practice. It sometimes helps to write more slowly. Find out the mistakes you are making and try to get into the habit of avoiding them. Get into good habits from the very start.

Writing: paragraphs

7.1 What is a paragraph?

A paragraph is **a group of sentences**. We divide a piece of writing into paragraphs in order to make it easier to read. We begin a new paragraph when there is a natural break in a piece of writing. Usually we are changing the subject in some way.

Imagine, for example, that you are writing a composition about your favourite sports and hobbies. You have decided to write about fishing, computer games, judo and tennis. This could sensibly be written as *four* paragraphs. What would be the subject of each paragraph?

1 _____

2 _____

3 _____

4 _____

Now do the same for the following topics.

a You are writing a description of some of your family. If you were to write a composition of *four* paragraphs, what might the subject of each paragraph be?

5 _____

6 _____

7 _____

8 _____

b You are writing a composition entitled 'The zoo'. If you divided the composition into four paragraphs, what might be the subject of each paragraph?

9 _____

10 _____

11 _____

12 _____

Answers can be found on page 28

7.2 Building a paragraph

A paragraph often begins with a sentence which tells us what the rest of the paragraph is going to be about. The rest of the sentences are then arranged in a sensible order so that the paragraph 'builds' in a logical way.

The eight sentences below can be used to make a single paragraph, but the order of the sentences needs to be changed. Arrange the sentences in the correct order, writing the letters in the spaces. The first one has been done for you.

a   I cannot remember it but my father says I was holding a rod when a fish suddenly started pulling on the line.

b   I started fishing when I was five years old.

c   I was so shocked I fell into the water.

d   I still go fishing with my father.

e   The hobby I enjoy most is fishing.

f   The experience didn't put me off as I have been fishing ever since.

g   We often go out on Sundays and spend the whole day fishing in the river.

h   That was when my father first took me fishing with him.

13 e _____	17 _____
14 _____	18 _____
15 _____	19 _____
16 _____	20 _____

7.3 Setting out paragraphs

The beginning of each paragraph should be a little way in from the margin. This makes it easier for the reader to see where each paragraph begins.

7.4 Paragraphs in stories

See the next topic (**Writing: stories**)

Answers can be found on page 28

Writing: stories

8.1 Planning

Stories are usually much more effective if you *plan* in advance what you are going to write. Stories which are not planned often become confused half-way through, or end too quickly. Planning a story means thinking about what you are going to write and about how you are going to organize your ideas. In particular, you should think about the following.

8.2 Setting

Where will your story take place? You might want to include a brief description of the setting. **When** do the events of the story happen? In the past? In the future? At night? In the morning?

8.3 Characters

Who will be in your story, and what will they be like? It is often a good idea to describe one or more of the characters. Can you think of *four* things you might want to tell the reader about a character?
One has been done for you.

1   Age
2   _____
3   _____
4   _____

8.4 Events

What happens in the story, and in what order do the events occur?

8.5 Beginning and ending

How will your story **begin**? Remember you want a good beginning to capture your reader's attention and interest. Think about stories that you

Answers can be found on page 29

have read, and how they started. Can you think of *four* different ways writers use to begin stories? One has been done for you.

> **5** Description of one of the characters
>
> **6** _____
>
> **7** _____
>
> **8** _____

How will your story **end**? Try not to end it too suddenly. Try to think of an ending that rounds the story off in a satisfying way.

8.6 Effect on reader

How do you want the person reading your story to react to it?
Think about stories you have read and the effect they have had on you.
Try to think of *four* different ways that the writer of a story might want the readers of the story to feel. Again, one has been done for you.

> **9** Excited
>
> **10** _____
>
> **11** _____
>
> **12** _____

8.7 Paragraphs in stories

As explained on pages 21–22, paragraphs are important in writing.
In story writing, here are some occasions when you might begin a new paragraph:

- when the setting changes (the story moves from one place to another)
- when a new character enters the story
- when the story moves forward in time.

If your story includes **conversations** between the characters, you should also start a new paragraph every time one character stops speaking and another character starts speaking.

Answers can be found on page 29

Writing: information writing

Information writing means writing that presents facts and information. In the Key Stage 2 Writing Test you will have the choice between writing a story or a piece of information writing. The information writing question, for example, might ask you to write a letter or a magazine or newspaper article.

9.1 Planning

Work out in advance the information you are going to include. In the Writing Test your question booklet will include a page on which you can write rough notes. You will also be given a few hints to help you think of ideas.

Arrange the points you are going to include in a sensible **order**. Imagine, for example, that you are writing to a pen-friend in another country about your school. Your rough notes might include ideas about the following:

a your thoughts about leaving the school and going to a new school
b basic facts about the school (what it is called, where it is, etc.)
c teachers in the school.

What would be the most sensible order for these points?
Write the letters (**a**, **b**, **c**) in order in the spaces below.

1 _____
2 _____
3 _____

Remember the points about **paragraphs** made on pages 21–22. Begin a new paragraph each time you change the subject in some way. The three ideas above, for example, could be written about in three separate paragraphs.

Answers can be found on page 29

9.2 Letter writing

The illustration below shows what a standard letter looks like.
Test your knowledge of letter writing by seeing if you know what should
go in the numbered spaces. Write your answers beneath the letter.
The first one has been done for you as an example.

```
                                                    (4)
                                    11 Haverhill Road
                                    Little Wratting
                                    Suffolk
                                    CB9 7UD

                                    ┌──────────────────┐
                                    │       (5)        │
                                    └──────────────────┘

                        (7)
┌──────────────────┐  ┌──────┐
│       (6)        │  │      │
└──────────────────┘  └──────┘


┌───────────────────────────────────────────────┐
│                                                 │
│                                                 │
│                                                 │
└───────────────────────────────────────────────┘


┌───────────────────────────────────────────────┐
│                                                 │
│                                                 │
│                                                 │
└───────────────────────────────────────────────┘

            ┌──────────────┐  (9)
            │     (8)      │  ┌──────┐
            └──────────────┘  └──────┘

                ┌──────────────┐
                │     (10)     │
                └──────────────┘
```

4 Your address   **8** _____

5 _____   **9** _____

6 _____   **10** _____

7 _____

Answers can be found on page 29

Reading

Here are some tips to help you prepare for the Reading Test.

10.1 Read!

The more you read, the better you will become at **understanding** what you read. Ask your parents and teachers for advice on what to read, and use your local library.

10.2 Think about what you read

This is what the questions in the Reading Test are really asking you to do. In particular, the Reading Test contains the following types of questions:

- **Questions which test your understanding**   If you are at home or at school and you find you are not properly understanding what you are reading, you could try reading more slowly or reading the passage again. You can also ask a parent or teacher for help.
- **Questions about characters**   Think about the characters in the stories that you read. What do you think of them? What in the story makes you think of them in this way?
- **Questions which ask your opinion**   At the end of a book or story, ask yourself why you have enjoyed it – or why you have not enjoyed it.

10.3 Enjoy your reading

Above all, reading should be a pleasure. If you enjoy a story by a particular writer, try to find other stories to read by the same writer.

A note to parents

You can help your children prepare for the Reading Test by reading books and stories with them and encouraging them to read independently. Ask your child questions about what they read.
The Reading Test questions in this book will give you an idea of the kind of questions to ask.

Answers to self-check questions

Topic 1 Grammar: parts of speech

1 It
2 He
3 I
4, 5 Possibly: wet/ muddy/dirty/untidy
6, 7 Possibly: angry/ cross/annoyed
8 jump or leap
9 slipped
10 fell
11 but
12 because
13 happiness
14 happy
15 angry
16 angrily
17 fright
18 frighteningly
19 courage
20 courageous

Topic 2 Grammar: sentences

1 Mary
2 The tree
3 The shop
4 Paul
5 he
6 his little sister
7 swam
8 fell
9 is
10 Correct
11 No verb
12 Correct
13 No verb
14 No subject
15 No subject
16 Correct
17 No verb
18 Correct
19 No subject
20 Correct

Topic 3 Punctuation

1 I
2 August
3 This
4 Sunday
5 I
6 Christopher
7 Laura
8 Robert
9 miles per hour
10 Mister
11 Doctor
12 Unidentified Flying Object
13 Member of Parliament
14 Question mark
15 Full stop
16 Full stop
17 Question mark
18 Full stop
19 Exclamation mark
20 Question mark

Topic 4 Punctuation continued

1 Kerry
2 nine
3 dresses
4 apples
5 oranges
6 bananas
7 Wendy's
8 friend's
9 women's
10 thieves'
11 Osborne's
12 pupils'
13 father's
14 James's
15 you're
16 can't
17 didn't
18 I'm 19
19 aren't
20 isn't

Topic 5 Spelling

1 foot-ball-er
2 in-ev-it-a-ble
3 dislike
4 was
5 beautiful
6 shining
7 brightly
8 there
9 telephone
10 answered
11 father
12 chemist's
13 said
14 work
15 early
16 meet
17 train
18 together
19 always
20 going

Topic 7 Writing: paragraphs

1 Fishing
2 Computer games
3 Judo
4 Tennis
5, 6, 7, 8 Possibilities include: your parents/brothers and sisters/your grandparents/ your aunts and uncles
9, 10, 11, 12 Possibilities include: lions and tigers/elephants/ chimpanzees/insects
13 **e**
14 **b**
15 **h**
16 **a**
17 **c**
18 **f**
19 **d**
20 **g**

Topic 8 Writing: stories

1 Age

2, 3, 4 Possibilities include: appearance/ personality/job or occupation/where the person lives

5 Description of one of the characters

6, 7, 8 Possibilities include: description of the setting/ description of an event (something happening)/with a conversation

9 Excited

10, 11, 12 Possibilities include: amused/ sad/curious

Topic 9 Writing: information writing

1 b

2 c

3 a

4 Your address

5 Date

6 Dear (with a capital *D*)

7 comma

8 sincerely (with a small *s*)

9 comma

10 Your signature

PART 2

Test practice papers

Taking the practice tests

Choose a place where your child will be comfortable and able to concentrate. It is best for your child to take the three Tests on different days. Before setting any of the Tests, read with your child through the **Instructions** at the beginning of the Test concerned.

The Reading Test

Give your child 15 minutes to read the three passages (the short story 'Ghostly Lessons', the leaflet about Newland Castle and the poem 'Two's Company'). Your child does not need to hurry because *they can look back at the passages during the Test*.

You should then give your child 45 minutes to answer the questions.

The Writing Test

Your child must choose whether to write a story or a letter – you might like to help them choose. You should then allow them 15 minutes to plan what they are going to write. Then give them another 45 minutes to write their answer.

The Spelling and Handwriting Test

The Spelling Test is explained on page 52. You need to read out a story to your child, whose version of the story on pages 52–53 misses out the words that they have to spell. This should take about ten minutes.

Immediately after the Spelling Test ask your child to copy out the passage on page 53 in their best handwriting. Allow five minutes for this.

Marking the questions

Detailed guidance on how to mark the questions begins on page 54. Your child will find it helpful if you explain the answers and how marks have been gained or lost.

Some answers are accompanied by a box containing a reference number, as in:

REF 5

This tells you the topic number you can refer to in Part 1 of this book to revise the material on which the question is based.

Marks can be entered on the Marking Grid on page 65. This also shows how your child's score can be converted into one of the **Levels** referred to on page 2.

Reading test

Instructions

- First spend 15 minutes reading the three passages. You then have 45 minutes to answer the questions.

- If you cannot answer a question, move on to the next one.
  If you have time, you can return to the question you found difficult later.

- In the Reading Test, you are asked to give *four* types of answer:

  - **Multiple-choice answers**
    Here the question is followed by four possible answers. Put a ring round the answer you think is correct.

  - **Single-line answers**
    Some questions are followed by a single line. This means your answer only needs to be one or two words, or a phrase.

  - **Several-line answers**
    Some questions are followed by two or three lines. This means you can write more words, or a sentence or two.

  - **Boxed answer**
    If a question is followed by a larger box, this means you should write a longer, more detailed answer.

- The numbers in brackets tell you how many marks are given for each question.

Answers can be found on pages 54–57

Here is a story about a ghost.

Ghostly Lessons

Lizzie, Paul, Molly and Lydia were cousins and the best of friends. Lizzie, who was eleven, was the oldest and the most sensible. Paul was nine and the most mischievous; he always knew how to make the others laugh. Molly, who was six, was the best swimmer and also had the loudest voice. Lydia was five and the best dancer.

They all lived with their families in the village of Prunton. Paul's family had only moved to the village recently and he had just started attending the local school. It was during his first week at the school that Paul had a very strange experience.

It was five o'clock in the afternoon and he was sitting in the kitchen, trying to do his Maths homework. His mother was just outside, hoovering the hall.

'Nine times forty nine,' he said out loud. 'Now then – nine nines are . . .'

'You should know that,' said a voice behind him. 'Eighty one'.

It was a lady's voice but when he looked behind him there was nobody there. He knew though that the voice had given him the right answer.

Paul spoke again. 'Who said that?'

'You can see me if you really want to,' said the voice. To Paul's amazement, a large white cloud suddenly appeared beside him. As Paul stared at it open-mouthed, it slowly changed shape and became an elderly lady, wearing glasses and dark, old-fashioned clothes. Paul was scared at first but the lady's twinkling eyes and warm smile somehow took away all his fear.

'Are you going to stare at me all day, or are you going to finish that sum?' the lady asked. 'Now, you've done the first part – oh, sorry, I'll have to be going.' The lady changed into a white cloud again and then disappeared just as Paul's mother came into the room.

Paul told his mother all that had happened. Of course she didn't believe a word of it. Paul had a reputation for practical jokes and his mother said that she knew a tall story when she heard one and this tale was taller than the Eiffel Tower.

His cousins reacted in the same way, at first. But when Paul insisted he was telling the truth they became more intrigued. Lydia was a little frightened to begin with, but Paul told her the ghost – if that was what it was – was kind and gentle.

Two days after Paul's strange experience, the cousins were having tea together with their grandmother. Lizzie, who had thought carefully about what Paul had told her, had come to the conclusion that if there really was a ghost in Paul's house, it was probably the ghost of someone who had once lived there. So she asked her grandmother, who had lived in the village all her life, about who had lived in the house before Paul and his parents.

'Let's see,' she replied. 'You remember the Websters, of course. They were a nice young family, weren't they? Then before them was Mr. Jenkins, a strange man who lived on his own with a lot of cats.'

'And before that?' asked Lizzie.

'Well, when I was growing up it was Miss Primrose's house. She was the village schoolteacher.'

Paul's eyes lit up and he looked across at Lizzie. 'What was she like?' he asked.

'She was a wonderful teacher,' his grandmother said. 'All the children loved her, even though she always wore dark clothes and was quite strict. She had lovely kind eyes and a beautiful smile.'

The next day was Saturday and Paul's parents were having a party to celebrate moving into their new house. The cousins waited until the grown-ups were together in the living-room then the four of them slipped quietly into the kitchen.

'Are you there, Miss Primrose?' asked Paul quietly.

All the children heard and saw what happened next. First they heard a lady's voice say 'Of course I am,' then a white cloud appeared in the corner of the room and finally the cloud changed into an old lady. The cousins stared at her.

'Don't be frightened,' she said. 'Won't you introduce me to your friends, Paul?'

'These are my cousins,' Paul explained. After he had told Miss Primrose his cousins' names, Molly, who was never frightened by anything, said in quite a loud voice, 'If you're so clever, what are thirteen thirteens?' Molly thought this was the hardest sum she had ever heard of, but she knew the answer because her father had told her at lunchtime.

'One hundred and sixty nine,' replied Miss Primrose, as quick as a flash.

'She's right!' gasped Mollie.

'And she didn't even use a calculator!' exclaimed Lizzie.

'What's a calculator?' Miss Primrose asked.

'I know what it is,' said Lydia. 'My daddy's got one. Come to my house and I'll show you.'

'Oh, I couldn't do that, I'm afraid,' Miss Primrose replied. 'But it's very kind of you to ask me. Now, have any of you got any homework you want me to help you with?'

'No,' said Paul. 'Today's Saturday and we're having a party.'

'How very nice. What about next week then?'

The cousins agreed to meet at Paul's house again on Monday and bring some homework with them. Paul had some more Maths, Lizzie had a story to write and Molly brought a reading book. Lydia wasn't quite sure what homework was but she brought a colouring book and some crayons.

They went into Paul's kitchen and called Miss Primrose's name. She appeared immediately and suggested they all go to the summerhouse in the garden.

The summerhouse had quite a lot of old furniture in it, including a big square table around which the cousins sat. They waited patiently until the familiar white cloud appeared and changed into Miss Primrose – they were getting quite used to it by now.

'I used to give lessons to my nephews and nieces in here,' said Miss Primrose. 'Look over there – I remember putting up that calendar myself.' On the wall was a calendar dated 1947.

After this lessons in the summerhouse became a regular event. Every afternoon after school the cousins would go there and Miss Primrose would help them with their sums and their reading. She even gave Molly advice on how to dive and taught Lydia some new dance steps. The children loved being with her, even though she once had to tell Paul off for trying to push a spider down the back of Molly's neck.

Their parents were puzzled and delighted by the cousins' behaviour. They agreed that they had never known such hardworking children.

Then one afternoon in the summerhouse Miss Primrose announced that this was to be their last lesson. The cousins immediately began to protest but Miss Primrose gently quietened them.

'If I carried on teaching you, it would be unfair on your schoolmates,' she explained. 'Now it's up to you to carry on working hard and prove that you can do well without any extra help. It's been wonderful getting to know you, and I hope you won't ever forget me.' And with that Miss Primrose smiled and for the very last time changed into a white cloud and disappeared.

The cousins were upset at first, but when they talked about it they agreed that they had been very lucky to have met Miss Primrose. They were sure they would never forget her. And once, at school, a strange thing happened to Paul as he was taking a test. He was trying to do a very hard question and felt like giving up. Suddenly he heard a familiar voice.

'Keep trying,' it said. 'You'll get there in the end.'

After that Paul carried on with the test, thinking that he would never feel like giving up again.

Here is a leaflet about a place to visit.

Newland Castle

Newland Castle is a genuine 16th-century castle which has been lovingly restored. But even if you've visited old castles before you'll never have been anywhere like Newland Castle. This is because Newland Castle uses the wonders of 20th-century technology to create an experience you'll never forget – the experience of being in the world's most haunted house!

In Newland Castle there's a ghost round every corner, sound effects to make your hair stand on end and tricks and illusions guaranteed to make your eyes pop out of your head in disbelief. Walk through walls and gaze in amazement at your friend's faces as they glow in the dark. See a floating staircase, furniture that moves around by  itself and statues that talk back when you speak to them. Struggle to stay on your feet in the amazing King's Bedroom, where the floor shakes and the walls are consumed by fire as thunder roars overhead.

Other attractions

After you've experienced the stunning technological wizardry of the main Castle building, you'll discover a different kind of magic in other parts of the Castle. Here you'll find rooms restored so that they look almost exactly as they must have done in the 16th century. Outside there are lovely grounds where you can walk or have a picnic. Or perhaps you'd rather hire a boat and row across the beautiful lake.

How to find us

As you can see from the map, we're easy to get to by car. Newland Castle is well signposted when you leave the M1 or M6 motorways. We are also only a mile from Newland train station. Buses from the station to the Castle run every 30 minutes.

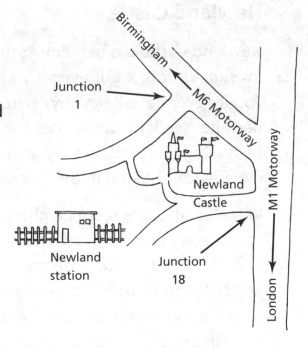

When to visit

Newland Castle is open every day of the year except Christmas Day and Boxing Day. Opening hours are from 9.30 am to 5.30 pm.

Ticket prices

Children (aged 14 or under)	£3
Adults	£7
Senior Citizens	£4
Family ticket (2 adults and up to 3 children)	£18

Note: Children under five are admitted free.

> *Visit Newland Castle – the heavily haunted home of a hundred ghosts!*

For more information ring 01786-265272

Here is a poem by Raymond Wilson called *Two's Company*.

Two's Company

They said the house was haunted, but
He laughed at them and said 'Tut, Tut!
I've never heard such tittle-tattle,
A ghost that groans and chains that rattle;
And just to prove I'm in the right,
Please leave me here to spend the night.'

They winked absurdly, tried to smother
Their ignorant laughter, nudged each other,
And left him just as dusk was falling
With a hunchback moon and screech owls calling –
Not that this troubled him one bit;
In fact, he was quite glad of it,
Knowing it's every sane man's mission
To contradict all superstition.

But what is that? Outside it seemed
As if chains rattled, someone screamed!
Come, come, it's merely nerves, he's certain
(But just the same he draws the curtain).
The stroke of twelve – but there's no clock!
He shuts the door and turns the lock
(Of course, he knows there's no one there,
But no harm is done by taking care!);
Someone's outside – the silly joker
(He may as well pick up the poker).
That noise again! He checks the doors,
Shutters the windows, makes a pause
To seek the safest place to hide –
(The cupboard's strong – he creeps inside).
'Not that there's anything to fear,'
He tells himself, when at his ear
A voice breathes softly, 'How-do-you-do!
I am the ghost. Pray, who are you?'

39

'Ghostly Lessons'

These questions are about the story 'Ghostly Lessons' on pages 32–36.

Put a ring around the group of words that best completes the sentences.

Q1 When Paul saw the ghost of Miss Primrose for the first time, he felt

| happy and curious | shocked and afraid | surprised and amused | excited and delighted |

Q1

Q2 After she has spoken to Paul for the first time, the ghost disappears because

| the sum is too difficult for her | she wants Paul to finish the sum | Paul's mother comes into the room | the sum is too easy |

Q2

Q3 Paul's mother thinks his story about the ghost is

| impossible to believe | very funny | very interesting | much too long |

Q3

Q4 When Paul tells his cousins about the ghost

| they laugh at him | they believe him, but not immediately | they immediately believe him | they are all very frightened |

1
Q4

Answers can be found on pages 54–57

Q5 Mr Jenkins was a man who lived in Paul's house

after Miss Primrose and before the Websters	after Miss Primrose and the Websters	before Miss Primrose and the Websters	before Miss Primrose and after the Websters

☐
1
Q5

Q6 The summerhouse in the garden of Paul's house

used to be the village school	was where Miss Primrose taught her own children	looked like a classroom	was where Miss Primrose used to teach some of her relatives

☐
1
Q6

Q7 The cousins' parents found the change in their children's behaviour

peculiar and worrying	surprising and annoying	strange but very pleasing	funny and unusual

☐
1
Q7

Q8 When Miss Primrose *announced that this was to be their last lesson* (page 35), the children

objected at first	were too upset to speak	did not argue	were very pleased

☐
1
Q8

These questions are about what happened in the story.

Q9 When Paul's grandmother explains that the old village schoolteacher, Miss Primrose, used to live in his house, *Paul's eyes lit up* (page 33). Why does he react in this way?

....

....

☐
1
Q9

Answers can be found on pages 54–57

Q10 The cousins' grandmother tells them that when she was a child Miss Primrose was the village schoolteacher. Write down two other points from the story which show that Miss Primrose was someone who lived many years ago.

....

....

2
Q10

Q11 The cousins' grandmother says that Miss Primrose was *quite a strict teacher*. Write down one occasion in the story when Miss Primrose shows that she is quite strict.

....

....

1
Q11

Q12 Lizzie is described as the most sensible of the cousins, while Paul is the most mischievous and Lydia is the youngest (page 32). Write down one example from the story of Lizzie being sensible, one example of Paul being mischievous, and one occasion when Lydia shows that she is the youngest.

1 Lizzie..

2 Paul...

3 Lydia..

3
Q12

Q13 Why are Molly and Lydia surprised when Miss Primrose knows the answer to Molly's question *'What are thirteen thirteens?'*

....

....

....

2
Q13

Answers can be found on pages 54–57

These questions are about how the story is written.

Q14 Paul's mother said that his story about having seen a ghost was *taller than the Eiffel Tower* (page 33). Why do you think she describes it in this way?

....

....

Q14

Q15 Paul tells Lydia that the ghost was kind and gentle (page 33). Find **two** words from the description of Paul's first meeting with the ghost which also show this.

....

2

Q15

Q16 Find **three** words from the story which show that Paul's grandmother liked Miss Primrose.

....

3

Q15

These questions ask you for your opinion of the story.

Q17 Do the cousins get on well with each other?

Yes [ ]   No [ ]

Explain your reasons, using parts of the story to help you.

....

....

....

....

3

Q17

Answers can be found on pages 54–57

Q18 Do you think Miss Primrose was right to stop giving lessons to the children?

Yes [ ]   No [ ]

Explain your reasons, using parts of the story to help you.

....

....

....

....

[ ]
3
Q18

Q19 The cousins were sure they would never forget Miss Primrose. Do you think they would ever forget her?

Yes [ ]   No [ ]

Explain your reasons, using parts of the story to help you.

....

....

....

....

[ ]
3
Q19

Newland Castle leaflet

These questions are about the Newland Castle leaflet on pages 37–38.

Q1 The ghosts at Newland Castle are not real. Write down *two* words from the leaflet which show this.

....

[ ]
2
Q1

Answers can be found on pages 54–57

Q2 The second paragraph of the leaflet refers to 'sound effects to make your hair stand on end'. Describe *two* sound effects which are mentioned in the leaflet.

1 ....

2 ....

`2`
Q2

Q3 Most people will visit Newland Castle to enjoy the experience of being in a house that appears to be haunted. According to the leaflet, there are other reasons for visiting the Castle as well. Describe *two* of these.

1 ....

....

2 ....

....

`2`
Q3

Q4 What is the main difference between the rooms mentioned in the Other Attractions section of the leaflet and the King's Bedroom mentioned earlier?

....

....

`1`
Q4

Q5 If you were travelling to Newland Castle from London by car, which motorway would you use?

....

`1`
Q5

Q6 Mr Jones, who is seventy-five years old, plans to visit Newland Castle with his two grandchildren – Peter, who is four, and Sally, who is ten. How much will each of their tickets cost?

`1`
Q6

1 Mr Jones .... 2 Peter .... 3 Sally ....

Answers can be found on pages 54–57

Q7 The leaflet says 'Visit Newland Castle – the heavily haunted home of a hundred ghosts!' The writer of the leaflet has tried to make this sentence funny and easy to remember. How have they done this?

....

....

`1`
Q7

Two's Company

These questions are about the poem *Two's Company* on page 39.

Q1 At the beginning of the poem the man is

sad and upset	confident and unafraid	angry and annoyed	worried and frightened

`1`
Q1

Q2 When the man is left at the house it is getting dark and there is 'a hunchback moon' in the sky. Why do you think the author describes the moon in this way?

....

....

`1`
Q2

Q3 When the man is inside the house, several scary things happen which make it seem as if the house is haunted. Write down *four* of these things.

1 ....

2 ....

3 ....

4 ....

`4`
Q3

Answers can be found on pages 54–57

Q4 In the last verse or section of the poem, certain parts are placed within brackets. An example is '(*But just the same he draws the curtain*).' Why do you think the author has separated these parts from the rest of the poem in this way?

....

....

....

....

2

Q4

Answers can be found on pages 54–57

Writing test

Instructions

- You have a choice of four different things to write about. You should choose just *one*. This means you must *either* write a story or a letter.
- You have 15 minutes to think about what you are going to write and to plan your answer. You can write brief notes during this time. If you choose to write a story, you should refer during this 15 minutes to **Story planning** on page 50. If you choose to write a letter, you should refer to **Letter planning** on page 51.
- You will then have 45 minutes to write your answer.

Story writing

Q1 **The Haunted House**

'Everyone said the house was haunted, but I found it hard to believe them. I decided to find out for myself.'

Write a short story, using this idea to help you.

You should think about:
- who is involved in the story
- what they do
- what happens to them.

Answers can be found on pages 58–61

Q2 **Moving House**

The story 'Ghostly Lessons' (in the Reading Test) begins soon after Paul's family have moved into a new home.

Write your own short story describing what happens when a family moves into a new house.

You should think about:
- who is in the story
- what their new house is like
- how the people in the story feel about moving.

Q3 **A Day Out**

Write a short story called 'A Day Out'.

You should think about:
- who is in the story
- where they go
- what happens.

Answers can be found on pages 58–61

Information writing

The family who live next door to you are moving. They have given you the address of the new family who will be moving into their house and have told you that the family include ten-year-old twins, Julie and Tony. Write a letter to either Julie or Tony, welcoming them to their new home.

Story planning

Use a piece of paper to plan your story. Make a brief note of some of your ideas, thinking in particular about:

Setting   (*Where does the story take place? When does it happen?*)

Characters (*Who is involved in the story? What are they like?*)

Events   (*What happens in the story?*)

Beginning   (*How will your story start?*)

End   (*How will your story end?*)

Answers can be found on pages 58–61

Letter planning

Use a piece of paper to plan your letter. Make a brief note of some of your ideas. You might find it helpful to think about:

- **How to set out your work**   (Remember that you should set out what you write as a letter.)
- **What information you are going to include in the letter**   You might, for example, want to say something about:
  - yourself
  - your family
  - your friends
  - your school
  - the street or area where you live.

Answers can be found on pages 58–61

Spelling and handwriting test

Spelling test instructions

- Parents should first refer to page 30.
- This Spelling Test will take about ten minutes.
- Part of a story called 'The House on the Hill' will be read out loud to you. You can follow the story by reading the version below, which has some words missing. When you hear the story for the first time, do not write anything.
- The story will then be read to you for a second time. When you come to an empty space in your version, wait until you hear the word and then write it in the space. If you are not sure how to spell a word, try to get as close as you can to what you think might be the correct spelling.

The House on the Hill

Mark Ashby lay on his bed _____ at the _____ .
He was bored. As _____ , he had arrived home from school at four o'clock and had something to eat. That was over an hour ago and now he could not think of anything to do.
The _____ passed more and more _____ . Mark _____ on his bed _____ six o'clock and then his older brother Colin came into his room and asked him if he wanted to go out. Colin said that he could not actually think of _____ to go, but that did not _____ Mark.
    It was a _____ evening and Mark and Colin both wished they had gone out earlier. It was still quite _____ but a gentle, refreshing _____ was blowing.
They _____ go to Frimley Hill, they decided. Frimley Hill was an area of open countryside that was only a few minutes away. At

Answers can be found on pages 62–63

the top of the hill was an old, deserted house. The roof had
_____ in and the windows were all broken.

As Mark and Colin _____ up the hill they saw the
house _____ of them. Mark saw something else as well and
when he pointed it out to Colin the two of them stopped and
stared up at the house. Through the gathering darkness they
could dimly make out a strange grey shape in one of the windows
– and it was _____ ! What they saw next _____ them
even more. Two piercing, luminous eyes _____ at the
window and stared _____ at them.

Handwriting test instructions

• Here is a short passage that continues the story from the Spelling
Test. Write it out as neatly as you can on a piece of paper, using
joined handwriting if you can. This should not take you more than
about five minutes.

Mark and Colin immediately turned away in terror. They
were about to run away when they heard a faint 'miaow'.
Looking back, they were just in time to see a small cat
leaping from the window, and a grey blanket gently
dropping to the ground behind it.

Answers can be found on pages 62–63

Answers: reading test

REF 10

Note: An asterisk (*) is used for each point which earns a mark, or part of a mark.

'Ghostly Lessons' (pages 32–36)

Questions 1–8

> **tip** *These are multiple choice questions. Advise your child always to consider each of the four possible answers. Sometimes one or two of the incorrect options are 'nearly right' and when the question is answered in a rush it is a common mistake to choose one of these rather than the correct option.*

Give 1 mark for each correct choice.
Q1 shocked and afraid*
Q2 Paul's mother comes into the room*
Q3 impossible to believe*
Q4 they believe him, but not immediately*
Q5 after Miss Primrose and before the Websters*
Q6 was where Miss Primrose used to teach some of her relatives*
Q7 strange but very pleasing*
Q8 objected at first*

`8`

Questions 9–16

Q9 Give 1 mark for an explanation along the following lines: the ghost acted like a schoolteacher so Paul now understood that it was probably the ghost of Miss Primrose.*

`1`

Q10 Give 1 mark each for any *two* of the following: Miss Primrose wears old fashioned clothes*/she does not know what a calculator is*/the calendar she put up in the summerhouse is dated 1947.*

`2`

Q11 Give 1 mark for an answer that refers to any *one* of the following: Miss Primrose tells Paul off for trying to push a spider down Molly's neck*/she says to Paul, 'Are you going to stare at me all day, etc.'*/she quietens the children down when they protest during the last lesson.*

`1`

Q12 Give 1 mark for each correct reference to the story. Maximum of 1 mark for each character. References must be associated with the right character.
Some possible references are listed below for each character. If other references are included which seem justified by a reading of the story, award a mark.

1 Lizzie: thinks carefully about what Paul told her*/realizes the ghost probably once lived in the house*/asks the grandmother about previous occupants of the house*

2 Paul: tries to push a spider down Molly's neck*/has a reputation for practical jokes*

3 Lydia: is frightened by Paul's story*/does not know what homework is*/wants to show the ghost her daddy's calculator*

`3`

Q13 Give 1 mark each for any *two* of the following points: Molly thinks the sum is very difficult*/Lizzie is surprised Miss Primrose can answer the question without using a calculator*/they are surprised at how quickly Miss Primrose answers*

`2`

Q14 Give 1 mark for an answer which shows an understanding that the mother thinks Paul has told her a tall story*, and that the story is compared to the Eiffel Tower because the Eiffel Tower is a very tall building*

`1`

Q15 Give 1 mark each for the following: twinkling*/warm*

`2`

Q16 Give 1 mark each for any *three* of the following: wonderful*/lovely*/kind*/beautiful*

`3`

Questions 17–19

tip *These questions ask about your child's opinion of the story. Although your child is asked to tick boxes marked 'Yes' or 'No', marks are **not** given for these ticks. This is because the answer is a matter of opinion. However, your child needs to give **reasons** for answering 'Yes' or 'No', and it is for this that marks are given.*

Q17 Give 1 mark if the answer refers to one detail or incident in the story which justifies the opinion given, 2 marks if it refers to two details or incidents and 3 marks if it refers to three or more details or incidents. Relevant references to the story include the following, but others are possible: the cousins are described as the best of friends*/Paul confides in the others about the ghost*/they keep the secret of the ghost to themselves*/they do things together*, e.g. tea with their grandmother, going to lessons with Miss Primrose/Paul knows how to make the others laugh*/Paul reassures Lydia when she is frightened by his story*/Paul tries to push a spider down Molly's neck* (this might be used as evidence of the cousins' playfulness *or* as evidence that they do not always get on well with each other).

`3`

Q18 Give 1 mark if the answer refers to the story in a vague, general way (e.g. *The lessons could not carry on forever*).*

Give 2 marks if the answer makes a more specific reference to the story** (e.g. it would be unfair on their schoolfriends if the lessons continued/Miss

Primrose now wanted the children to prove that they could work hard without extra help).

Give 3 marks if the answer makes two or more specific references to the story.***

`3`

Q19 Give 1 mark if an opinion is expressed but no reason is given (e.g. *I think they will always remember her*).

Give 2 marks if the answer justifies the opinion by reference to events in the story or to particular aspects of it** (e.g. they will never forget seeing a ghost/they will never forget Miss Primrose because she was very kind to them).

Give 3 marks if the answer shows an understanding of the moral at the end of the story – that Miss Primrose has taught the children the virtues of hard work and perseverance, and this will remain with them.***

`3`

Total marks available: 32

Newland Castle leaflet (pages 37–38)

Q1 Give 1 mark each for any *two* of the following: tricks*/illusions*/technological*/wizardry*

`2`

Q2 Give 1 mark for each of the following: statues which reply when spoken to*/the sound of thunder overhead in the King's Bedroom*

`2`

Q3 Give 1 mark each for any *two* of the following: historical interest (restored rooms, etc.)*/lovely grounds*/pleasant walks*/a place to have a picnic*/beautiful lake*/opportunity to hire a rowing boat*

`2`

Q4 Give 1 mark for any explanation along the following lines: The King's Bedroom is one of the rooms that has been made to appear haunted. The other rooms have been restored so they look as they did in the past. They are not haunted.*

`1`

Q5 MI*

`1`

Q6 Give 1 mark only if each ticket price has been correctly identified:
Mr Jones – £4*/Peter – Free*/Sally – £3*

`1`

Q7 Give 1 mark if the answer recognizes that the sentence contains several words beginning with the letter *h*.* (The technical term for this is alliteration, but the answer does not have to use this term.)

`1`

Total marks available: 10

'Two's Company' (page 39)

Q1   confident and unafraid*

1

Q2   Give 1 mark for any answer which refers to the **shape** of the moon* (e.g. that it is **curved**, or that there is a **half-moon**). Alternatively, the answer may say that the description helps to give the poem a frightening atmosphere – 1 mark can be given for this.

1

Q3   Give 1 mark each for any *four* of the following: chains rattle*/someone screams*/there is no clock but the sound of a clock striking is heard*/it sounds as if someone is outside*/in the cupboard a ghost speaks to the man.*

4

Q4   The parts in brackets describe the man's reactions to the strange things that happen.* These reactions show that he is really afraid, although pretending not to be.* Give 2 marks for a clear explanation of both these points. Give 1 mark for a less clear or an incomplete explanation.

2

Total marks available: 8

Answers: writing test

REF 8, 9

tip *Although no marks are given for the notes your child makes during the 15 minutes planning time, you can check that your child has made constructive use of this time. Children almost always score higher marks if they have a clear idea of what they are going to write before they begin writing the actual answer.*

In the National Tests, your child's writing is assessed under two broad headings:

1 **Purpose and Organization**   This refers to **what** your child has written. Is it interesting, relevant and well organized?

2 **Grammar**   This refers to **how** your child has written his or her answer. For the purposes of assessment, grammar is subdivided into **punctuation** (the correct use of full stops, commas and so on) and **style** (how well your child's ideas are expressed).

Marks

Your child's piece of writing should be marked out of 35. Marks are allocated as follows:

Purpose and Organization   21
Grammar: punctuation   7
Grammar: style   7
                          ___
                           35

The tables on the next few pages show how to award marks in more detail. Different Levels of achievement are described, and for each Level the appropriate mark is given. For each of the three headings mentioned above, you should read the descriptions of the kinds of writing that should be awarded particular marks. When you have found the description that best fits your child's writing, give the corresponding mark. Add up the three marks to find the total out of 35.

Do not worry if your child's work does not match a Level description in every particular. Remember you are looking for the description which *best fits* what your child has written. You might also find that your child is not at the same Level for everything. For example, he or she might be Level 3 for punctuation and Level 4 for style. This does not necessarily mean you have marked inaccurately. It does, however, help you to identify the strengths and weaknesses of your child's writing.

Purpose and organization

Story writing
- The writing has some of the basic structure expected of a story: a clear beginning, more than one character and a sequence of two or more events.
- Events and characters are not described in any detail.

Letter writing
- Some basic aspects of a simple letter format are present.
- Some relevant points are made but they are not developed or connected.

Story writing
- The story is sensibly organized, with a beginning, a middle and a simple but appropriate ending.
- Several events are presented in a logical sequence.
- Some details are included in the descriptions of characters and settings.

Letter writing
- A simple letter format is used.
- The letter begins in a sensible way and the points made are presented in a logical sequence.
- Some of the points made are explained in more detail to make them more interesting to the reader.

Story writing
- The story is well paced (e.g. there may be a successful attempt to create excitement or suspense).
- Characters are more fully developed and there is some interaction between them.
- The story is readable and tries to arouse the reader's interest.

Letter writing
- Most of the conventions associated with a letter format are present.
- The letter begins and ends well, and the points made during the letter are logically connected and developed.
- A clear attempt is made to engage the interest of the reader.

Story writing

- The story is well structured.
- Different story-telling techniques may be used (e.g. dialogue, action, description) and these are effectively combined.
- Paragraphs are used to separate the main stages of the story (e.g. beginning, middle and end).

Letter writing

- All of the conventions associated with a letter format are present.
- The letter makes sensible points, which are well organized and explained in sufficient detail. Paragraphs are used to separate the main stages of the letter.
- The letter addresses the reader in an appropriate tone throughout.

LEVEL 5

18 marks

Story writing

- The story is well constructed and has a central theme (idea) running through it, as well as a clearly developed plot (sequence of events).
- Characters and events are very effectively presented, successfully using a range of techniques (e.g. dialogue, description).
- Paragraphs are used correctly and are used in the presentation of dialogue.

Letter writing

- All the conventions associated with a letter format are present.
- The letter begins and ends strongly. Points are relevant, clearly explained and well organized. Paragraphs are used correctly throughout.
- The reader is addressed in an appropriate tone and the writer makes a clear, successful attempt to engage the reader's interest.

HIGH LEVEL 5

21 marks

Grammar: punctuation

- Capital letters and full stops are used correctly in a few places.

BELOW LEVEL 3

2 marks

- At least half the sentences show the correct use of capital letters, full stops and question marks.

LEVEL 3

2 marks

- The majority of sentences show the correct use of capital letters, full stops and question marks.
- There is some correct use of commas, and inverted commas (speech marks) are used for direct speech.

LEVEL 4

5 marks

LEVEL 5	<ul><li>Almost all sentences show the correct use of capital letters, full stops and question marks.</li><li>Commas and speech marks are correctly used.</li><li>A wider range of punctuation (e.g. brackets, dashes) is used.</li></ul>

6 marks

HIGH LEVEL 5	<ul><li>All punctuation marks are accurately used.</li><li>A wide range of punctuation is used.</li><li>Punctuation increases the effectiveness of the writing (e.g. by varying pace).</li></ul>

7 marks

Grammar: style

BELOW LEVEL 3	<ul><li>Sentences are simple, and tend to resemble speech (e.g. 'and' and 'then' are frequently used to link sentences).</li><li>Vocabulary is simple, and again resembles that used in speech (e.g. use of 'thing', 'get', 'make').</li></ul>

2 marks

LEVEL 3	<ul><li>Some use of conjunctions (e.g. 'because', 'but', 'when').</li><li>Some use of adverbs (e.g. 'quickly', 'carefully').</li></ul>

4 marks

LEVEL 4	<ul><li>Longer, more complex sentences are used, with a wider range of conjunctions (e.g. 'although', 'however').</li><li>Vocabulary is more varied and descriptions include interesting, well-chosen words.</li><li>Tenses (e.g. past or present) are used consistently throughout.</li></ul>

5 marks

LEVEL 5	<ul><li>Writing is interesting and varied, with appropriate use of both short and long sentences.</li><li>Choice of words is imaginative and has an appropriate level of formality or informality.</li></ul>

6 marks

HIGH LEVEL 5	<ul><li>The writing is expressive and effective throughout.</li><li>There may be some imaginative and adventurous use of language, including the use of devices such as onomatopoeia (e.g. 'the thunder **rumbled** on') or alliteration (e.g. 'he **raged** and **ranted**').</li></ul>

7 marks

Answers: spelling test

REF 5

The passage below is the one you should read out to your child (see page 27). Read it once to your child without stopping. Then read it a second time, pausing each time you reach one of the words in **bold print**. Ask your child to write down each word in the spaces on pages 52–53. (You will find this easier if you copy the passage out beforehand, so you are able to read it out while your child fills in the blank spaces.)

The House on the Hill

Mark Ashby lay on his bed **staring** at the **ceiling**. He was bored. As **usual**, he had arrived home from school at four o'clock and had something to eat. That was over an hour ago and now he could not think of anything to do. The **minutes** passed more and more **slowly**. Mark **remained** on his bed **until** six o'clock and then his older brother Colin came into his room and asked him if he wanted to go out. Colin said that he could not actually think of **anywhere** to go, but that did not **worry** Mark.

It was a **beautiful** evening and Mark and Colin both wished they had gone out earlier. It was still quite **warm** but a gentle, refreshing **breeze** was blowing. They **would** go to Frimley Hill, they decided. Frimley Hill was an area of open countryside that was only a few minutes away. At the top of the hill was an old, deserted house. The roof had **fallen** in and the windows were all broken.

As Mark and Colin **climbed** up the hill they saw the house **ahead** of them. Mark saw something else as well, and when he pointed it out to Colin the two of them stopped and stared up at the house. Through the gathering darkness they could dimly make out a strange grey shape in one of the windows – and it was **moving**! What they saw next **startled** them even more. Two piercing, luminous eyes **appeared** at the window and stared **directly** at them.

Marks

Use the table below to find out how many marks your child has scored in the Spelling Test.

Number of correct words	Spelling test mark
1–2	1
3–4	2
5–6	3
7–8	4
9–10	5
11–12	6
13–14	7
15–16	8
17–18	9
19–20	10

tip *Encourage your child to keep a list of words that he or she spells incorrectly (see page 18).*

Answers: handwriting test

REF 6

To mark your child's Handwriting Test, look at the table below. You need to decide which description and which sample of handwriting corresponds most closely to your child's handwriting. Do not expect there to be an exact resemblance – you are looking for the description which *best fits* your child's handwriting.

Mark and Colin immediately turned away in terror. They were about to turn away when they heard a faint 'miaow'.

1 mark

Handwriting legible but size and shape of letters is inconsistent. Spaces between words and letters is also inconsistent. Handwriting is not joined.

Mark and Colin immediately turned away in terror. They were about to turn away when they heard a faint 'miaouw'.

2 marks

Most letters correctly formed. Size and shape of most letters consistent. Most words and letters are spaced correctly. Handwriting is not joined.

Mark and Colin immediately turned away in terror. They were about to turn away when they heard a faint 'miaow'!

3 marks

All letters correctly formed. Size and shape of all letters consistent. Most words and letters are spaced correctly. Words are clearly printed or partially joined.

Mark and Colin immediately turned away in terror. They were about to turn away when they heard a faint 'miaow'.

4 marks

Joined handwriting is used. Letters are joined in a consistent and appropriate way. All words and letters are spaced correctly.

Mark and Colin immediately turned away in terror. They were about to turn away when they heard a faint 'miaow'.

5 marks

Handwriting is mature, clear and confident and correct throughout.

Marking grid

Reading (pages 31–37)

Question	Marks available	Marks scored
Reading Test (*Ghostly Lessons*)	32	
Reading Test (Newland Castle)	10	
Reading Test (*Two's Company*)	8	
total	50	

Writing (pages 48–51)

Question	Marks available	Marks scored
Writing Test: Purpose and Organization	21	
Writing Test: Punctuation	7	
Writing Test: Style	7	
Spelling Test	10	
Handwriting Test	5	
total	50	

What the results mean

	Reading	Writing	Reading + writing
Maximum mark	50	50	100
Below Level 3	0–15	0–25	0–41
Level 3	16–25	26–33	42–59
Level 4	26–35	34–41	60–77
Level 5	36–45	42–49	78–95
High Level 5	46–50	50	96–100

Mark scored in Reading Test [ ] ▶ Level [ ]

Mark scored in Writing Test [ ] ▶ Level [ ]

Total [ ] ▶ Level [ ]

Note: These Levels are explained on page 2. Level 4 is the typical result achieved by an 11-year-old. Level 3 means the child's achievement is slightly below average. Level 5 is above average.